CLEAN
EATING

igloobooks

Published in 2016
by Igloo Books Ltd
Cottage Farm
Sywell
NN6 0BJ
www.igloobooks.com

Following images are courtesy of ©Shutterstock:
4 © PageSteven/Shutterstock, 7b © Alena Haurylik/Shutterstock, 8b © Losangela/Shutterstock,
11t © Adisa/Shutterstock, 12 © Elena Veselova/Shutterstock, 30 © Simon Booth/Shutterstock,
46 © Rustle/Shutterstock, 62 © Dani Vincek/Shutterstock
All additional images iStock/Getty

Cover and interiors designed by Nicholas Gage
Edited by Natalie Baker

LEO002 1116
2 4 6 8 10 9 7 5 3 1
ISBN 978-1-78670-253-1

Printed and manufactured in China

Contents

Going Clean

Clean eating breaks many of the rules of traditional dieting and offers a long-term healthy-eating solution, which focuses purely on nutrition and eating whole foods. This means that there is no calorie counting or reading the labels of processed foods. In fact, processed foods are out; whole, natural and unrefined foods are in.

Limit processed foods

Research on food habits has shown that the processed-food revolution, which started in the 1970s, correlates to the increased obesity levels we have seen over the last 40 years. As consumers have become reliant on cheap, convenient foods, they have lost their cooking skills and reduced their healthy nutrient intake. This has led to increased consumption of high sugar, high salt and additive-rich food products. Clean eating is about finding recipes and meals that can replace these processed foods with more natural, nutrient-dense alternatives. This book provides you with a number of suggestions for all your meals and snacks, and offers a head start for your new healthy-eating regime.

Healthy digestion

A healthy body starts with a healthy digestive system – we are not what we eat but what we absorb. Our digestive tract is a delicate and complex organ that needs to be taken care of so that we can gain all the benefits from the foods we eat. Factors such as stress, alcohol, smoking and poor diet can all lead to damage of the intestinal lining and can disturb the balance of bacterial microflora within the gut. By reducing the number of refined foods and alcohol you consume, and increasing the prebiotic and probiotic foods in your diet, you can improve your digestive health.

Going free-from

Increases in the prevalence of food intolerances have been apparent in recent years as more people start to notice the impact that certain foods have on the way they feel. Some people find that following a gluten- or dairy-free diet makes them feel less bloated, for example. Clean eating is about finding natural foods that complement your body. If you choose to cut out certain food groups completely, these foods need to be replaced with healthy alternatives that offer you the same nutrients.

Making time to eat

Living in such a fast-paced society where we rush our food and skip meals could also be making us feel ill. Setting time aside to sit down to eat is important. It gives your body time to properly digest your food. Chewing your food is the first stage in the digestive process, so rushing this means that your gut needs to work much harder to try to extract those essential nutrients.

How will you feel?

'Energetic' and 'healthy' are just some of the words used to describe how people feel once they clean up their eating habits. This style of eating requires more preparation time and a little inspiration, but this book aims to provide you with all the tools you need to get started.

What's really clean?

It can be difficult to keep up with the vast array of new ingredients that are flooding our shops and farmers markets. The guide below aims to help you decide which ingredients to try and what they might replace in your current diet. Whatever you replace, keep it simple and close to its most natural form.

Starchy foods

Bread, cereals, rice and pasta form the basis of many of our meals and provide your body with energy, fibre, essential B vitamins, iron, calcium and folate. Processed versions of these foods are stripped of their fibre and nutrient content, and so it is important to include as many wholegrain cereals as you can. Empty carbohydrates made from refined flour all contribute to spiked blood sugar levels and energy slumps. To maintain your energy levels throughout the day, choose foods that slowly release sugars into your blood. These are the more complex, fibre-containing carbohydrates, such as oats.

Out – white bread, white pasta, white rice and refined cereals

In – wholegrain bread, wholemeal pasta, brown rice and gluten-free grains

Fruit and vegetables

Making fruit and vegetables the main part of each meal is the essence of clean eating. These foods provide us with a rich assortment of vitamins, minerals, fibre, antioxidants and other phytonutrients that nourish our body and keep our digestive system healthy.

Out – pesticide and fungicide-sprayed fruits and vegetables, transported from around the globe

In – organic, local and seasonal produce

Protein

Less meat and more sustainable options are the main messages when choosing proteins. Try to include some meat-free days, replacing meat with plant-based proteins, such as nuts and lentils. Fish, particularly oily fish such as mackerel that contain omega 3 fatty acids, are great mood foods. Increased levels of omega 3 fats have also been found to reduce inflammation in the body.

Out – processed meats such as packaged ham, chicken, corned beef, salami and sausages

In – sustainably-caught seafood, free-range eggs and poultry, unprocessed and unsalted nuts, beans, lentils and pulses

Fats and oils

Fats and oils are an essential part of our diet. They are responsible for helping to keep our skin healthy and for transporting fat soluble vitamins A, D, E and K around our body. You do, however, want all the benefits of healthy fats without the negative impact of consuming refined oils. Pure oils such as extra virgin olive oil or avocado oil provide our body with mono- and polyunsaturated fatty acids.

Out – hydrogenated fats, low-fat spreads and refined oils such as palm or canola oil

In – unrefined oils such as extra virgin olive oil, safflower, avocado, coconut and almond oil

Dairy and dairy-free alternatives

As the movement towards dairy-free diets builds momentum, so too does the range of dairy alternatives. From soya and almond milk to cashew nut butter and home-made coconut butter, the option to eat 'clean' foods is much more accessible. Tofu is a great alternative to cheese and can be added to meals to boost your protein intake.

Out – processed cheese, processed cow's milk, yogurts, crème fraîche and cream

In – organic dairy foods, unprocessed dairy alternatives

Clean up and clear out

So you've decided that you're ready to start eating clean. Any kind of lifestyle change can be daunting at first but with some preparation and planning, the process can be made as simple as the food itself.

Store cupboard essentials

Wholegrain cereals such as brown rice, oats, buckwheat, couscous, millet or quinoa

Dried herbs and spices

Canned or dried chickpeas, beans and lentils

Canned fruit in natural juices

Sun-dried tomatoes

Unsulphured dried fruit

Wholemeal or gluten-free flour

Maple syrup

Unrefined oils

Unflavoured, unsalted nuts

Cleanse your cupboards

The first stage of eating clean is to clear out or use up any processed foods you have. Remove any foods that are not in their natural state, including tinned foods such as baked beans, shop-bought sauces, packet mixes, and ready meals. You may find that after your clear out you have a lot more space in your cupboards. However, be aware that you'll be replacing the processed foods with fresh ingredients that will need to be stored in a cool, dry place.

Where and how to shop

With clean eating comes shopping for fresh, natural ingredients that won't last as long without the added preservatives. There are, however, several things you can do to make shopping and cooking with fresh produce more convenient. Identify where you plan to buy your fresh fruit and vegetables – you could visit a farmers market or even grow your own produce. Fresh fruit and vegetables will only last a few days in the fridge, so plan what you're going to eat for the week before you buy the produce.

Batch cooking

Prevent wasting fresh food by batch cooking once a week. This is a great way to preserve the nutritional value of your ingredients. Batch cooking also makes cooking during the week more convenient. Batch cooking is essential if you want to eat seasonally because most fruit and vegetables can be harvested only between spring and early autumn, and so freezing is vital if you want to enjoy these foods through the winter months.

Storage of ingredients

Wholegrains contain natural oils that can go rancid quickly. Store grains in airtight containers, such as sealed glass jars, in a cool, dark place. If stored correctly, they can last for three to six months. The same rule should also be applied to unrefined oils, which are particularly susceptible to oxidation.

Breakfast

Choosing a meal full of fresh, unprocessed foods in their most natural state is a great way to begin the day. Real foods offer a really beneficial daily boost of energy while helping to improve your concentration and performance. Consuming food the way nature intended, or at least as close to it as possible, is the mantra on the Clean Eating diet and it really is so quick and easy to prepare a nutritious, energy-boosting breakfast using unrefined foods. For example, fruits, nuts and fresh low-fat, gluten-free produce are generally readily accessible and provide a joyous way to jump-start a busy day. The **Smashed Avocado on Toast** is super simple and delicious, or why not try the **Berry Smoothie Bowl** for a fantastic, filling meal? It is important to take time for breakfast and not be tempted to skip this first meal of the day. Your general health and wellbeing will improve once you maintain a routine that begins with a nourishing meal and, with plenty of suggestions in the following recipes on how to create inspirational yet simple breakfasts, there are really no excuses!

Smashed Avocado on Toast

SERVES: **4** - PREP. TIME: **5 MINS** / COOKING TIME: **4 MINS**

INGREDIENTS

4 slices wholegrain bread

2 ripe avocados, halved and stoned

1 lime, juiced

2 spring onions (scallions), very finely chopped

tomato, cucumber or fried quails' eggs to serve

flat leaf parsley to garnish

METHOD

- Toast the bread under a hot grill until crisp on both sides.
- Meanwhile, scoop the avocado flesh into a bowl and mash roughly with a fork, incorporating the lime juice and spring onion as you go. Season to taste with salt and pepper.
- Spread the avocado onto the toast, add the toppings of your choice and garnish with parsley.

Matcha and Chia Smoothie

SERVES: **2** - PREP. TIME: **25 MINS** / COOKING TIME: **0 MINS**

INGREDIENTS

50 g / 1 ¾ oz / ¼ cup chia seeds
1 tbsp matcha green tea powder
600 ml / 1 pint / 2 ½ cups soya milk
2 bananas, sliced and frozen for at least 2 hours
2 tbsp maple syrup
1 tbsp goji berries

METHOD

- Stir the chia seeds and matcha into the soya milk and leave to thicken for 20 minutes.
- Transfer to a liquidiser with the bananas and maple syrup and blend until smooth.
- Pour into two glasses and serve immediately, garnished with goji berries.

Blueberry and Tofu Smoothie

SERVES: 2 - PREP. TIME: **5 MINS** / FREEZING TIME: **2 HOURS**

INGREDIENTS

150 g / 5 ½ oz / 1 cup blueberries

100 g / 3 ½ oz / ½ cup silken tofu

350 ml / 12 fl. oz / 1 ½ cups pure blueberry juice

1 tbsp runny honey

2 sprigs mint

METHOD

- Reserve a few blueberries for garnish then spread the rest out on a baking tray and freeze for at least 2 hours. They can then be stored in a freezer bag for later use or used straight away.
- Put the frozen blueberries in a liquidiser with the tofu, juice and honey and blend until very smooth.
- Pour into two glasses, garnish with blueberries and mint and serve immediately.

Mushroom and Tofu Galettes

SERVES: 4 - PREP. TIME: **2 HOURS 15 MINS** / COOKING TIME: **25 MINS**

INGREDIENTS

200 g / 7 oz extra-firm tofu, in 1 piece

1 tbsp sea salt

3 tbsp extra virgin olive oil

150 g / 5 ½ oz / 2 cups mushrooms, sliced

1 tbsp fresh thyme leaves

2 cloves of garlic, crushed

a few chives to garnish

baby spinach and cherry tomatoes to serve

FOR THE GALETTE BATTER:

75 g / 2 ½ oz / ½ cup buckwheat flour

1 large egg

150 ml / 5 ½ fl. oz / 2/3 cup soya or almond milk

1 tbsp coconut oil, melted, plus extra for frying

METHOD

- Sprinkle the tofu all over with salt, then sandwich it between two double layers of kitchen paper and weigh it down with a heavy wooden chopping board. Leave for 2 hours or preferably overnight.
- To make the galette batter, put all of the ingredients in a liquidiser and blend until smooth. Rest the batter in the fridge for at least 2 hours or preferably overnight.
- Grease a crepe pan with coconut oil and set it over a medium heat. Add a ladle of batter and swirl to coat the base of the pan. Cook for 1–2 minutes on each side then repeat with the rest of the batter to form four galettes. Keep warm.
- Heat the olive oil in a sauté pan and fry the mushrooms and thyme with a pinch of salt for 10 minutes. Add the garlic and sauté for 2 minutes.
- Divide the mushrooms between the galettes and crumble over the salted tofu. Garnish with chives and fold in the edges, then serve with baby spinach and cherry tomatoes.

Green Fruit Smoothie Bowl

SERVES: 2 - PREP. TIME: 15 MINS / FREEZING TIME: 2 HOURS

INGREDIENTS

3 bananas

3 kiwi fruit, peeled

150 g / 5 ½ oz / 1 cup blueberries

3 green apples, cored and thinly sliced

35 g / 1 ¼ oz / 1 cup young kale

35 g / 1 ¼ oz / 1 cup baby leaf spinach

250 ml / 9 fl. oz / 1 cup coconut milk

250 ml / 9 fl. oz / 1 cup apple juice

2 tbsp maple syrup

1 lime, cut into thin wedges

2 tbsp toasted oats

1 tbsp desiccated coconut

a few sprigs mint

METHOD

- Set aside a banana and a kiwi for the garnish then peel and chop the rest. Spread half the blueberries, two of the sliced apples and the chopped banana and kiwi out on a greaseproof paper lined baking tray and freeze for at least 2 hours. The fruit can then be transferred to a freezer bag and stored for future use or used straight away.

- Put the kale and spinach in a liquidiser with the coconut milk, apple juice and maple syrup. Blend until smooth.

- Add the frozen fruit and blend again until smooth, then pour into two chilled bowls.

- Cut the final kiwi in half in a zigzag pattern, then peel and slice the final banana. Arrange on top of the smoothie with the blueberries, apple and lime slices, then sprinkle with oats and coconut. Garnish with mint and serve immediately.

Banana and Almond Smoothie

SERVES: **2** - PREP. TIME: **5 MINS** / FREEZING TIME: **2 HOURS**

INGREDIENTS

2 bananas, sliced

500 ml / 17 ½ fl. oz / 2 cups almond milk

1 tbsp runny honey

METHOD

- Spread the banana slices out on a baking tray and freeze for at least 2 hours. They can then be stored in a freezer bag for later use or used straight away.
- Put the frozen banana in a liquidiser with the almond milk and honey and blend until very smooth.
- Pour into two glasses and serve immediately.

Quinoa Granola

SERVES: 6 - PREP. TIME: 5 MINS / COOKING TIME: 1 HOUR

INGREDIENTS

75 ml / 2 ½ fl. oz / 1/3 cup runny honey

75 ml / 2 ½ fl. oz / 1/3 cup apple juice

1 tbsp extra virgin olive oil

175 g / 6 oz / 1 ¾ cups rolled porridge oats

100 g / 3 ½ oz / ¾ cup almonds, roughly chopped

75 g / 2 ½ oz / ½ cup quinoa

50 g / 1 ¾ oz / ½ cup sunflower seeds

200 g / 7 oz / 1 cup goji berries

10 medjool dates, stoned and chopped

METHOD

- Preheat the oven to 160°C (140°C fan) / 325F / gas 3.

- Stir the honey, apple juice and oil together in a bowl with a pinch of salt then toss it with the oats, almonds, quinoa and sunflower seeds.

- Spread the mixture out on a large baking tray and bake for 1 hour, stirring every 10 minutes to ensure it all toasts evenly. Leave the granola to cool completely, then stir in the goji berries and dates.

- Store in an airtight jar until needed.

Raspberry and Oat Smoothie

SERVES: **2** - PREP. TIME: **2 HOURS 5 MINS** / COOKING TIME: **0 MINS**

INGREDIENTS

150 g / 5 ½ oz / 1 cup raspberries

300 ml / 10 ½ fl. oz / 1 ¼ cups almond milk

50 g / 1 ¾ oz / ½ cup rolled porridge oats, plus extra for sprinkling

1 tbsp runny honey

METHOD

- Spread out the raspberries on a baking tray that has been lined with greaseproof paper and freeze for at least 2 hours.
- Meanwhile, put the almond milk and oats in a liquidiser and leave to soak.
- When the raspberries are ready, transfer them to the liquidiser with the honey and blend until smooth.
- Pour into two jars or glasses and serve with a sprinkle of oats on top.

Mean Green Juice

SERVES: **2** - PREP. TIME: **5 MINS** / FREEZING TIME: **2 HOURS**

INGREDIENTS

2 sticks celery, chopped

150 g / 5 ½ oz / 1 cup apples, peeled, cored and cubed

150 g / 5 ½ oz / 1 cup green seedless grapes

35 g / 1 ¼ oz / 1 cup spinach

35 g / 1 ¼ oz / 1 cup flat-leaf parsley

500 ml / 18 fl. oz / 2 cups apple juice

1 lemon, juiced

METHOD

- Spread the celery, apple and grapes out on a greaseproof paper lined baking tray and freeze for at least 2 hours. It can then be transferred to a freezer bag and stored for future use or used straight away.
- Put the spinach and parsley in a liquidiser with the apple juice and lemon juice. Blend until smooth.
- Add the frozen celery, apple and grapes and blend again until smooth, then pour into glasses and serve immediately.

Berry Smoothie Bowl

SERVES: 2 - **PREP. TIME: 25 MINS** / COOKING TIME: **0 MINS**

INGREDIENTS

50 g / 1 ¾ oz / ¼ cup chia seeds

28 g / 1 oz / ¼ cup buckwheat porridge flakes

500 ml / 17 ½ fl. oz / 2 cups almond milk

150 g / 5 ½ oz / 1 cup frozen summer berries

2 tbsp maple syrup

TO GARNISH:

1 handful fresh berries

2 tbsp goji berries

2 tbsp chia seeds

2 tbsp pumpkin seeds

2 tbsp sunflower seeds

METHOD

- Stir the chia seeds and buckwheat flakes into the almond milk and leave to thicken for 20 minutes.
- Transfer to a liquidiser and add the berries and maple syrup and blend until very smooth.
- Pour into two bowls and arrange the berries and seeds on top.

Avocado Spinach Smoothie

SERVES: **2** - PREP. TIME: **5 MINS** / FREEZING TIME: **2 HOURS**

INGREDIENTS

2 ripe avocados, skinned, stoned and chopped

1 banana, chopped

35 g / 1 ¼ oz / 1 cup baby leaf spinach

250 ml / 9 fl. oz / 1 cup soya milk

½ lemon, juiced

METHOD

- Spread the avocado and banana out on a greaseproof paper lined baking tray and freeze for at least 2 hours. It can then be transferred to a freezer bag and stored for future use or used straight away.
- Put the spinach in a liquidiser with the soya milk and lemon juice. Blend until smooth.
- Add the frozen avocado and banana and blend again until smooth, then pour into two glasses and serve immediately.

Hazelnut and Cherry Granola

SERVES: **6** - PREP. TIME: **5 MINS** / COOKING TIME: **1 HOUR**

INGREDIENTS

75 ml / 2 ½ fl. oz / 1/3 cup maple syrup

75 ml / 2 ½ fl. oz / 1/3 cup white grape juice

1 tbsp linseed oil

175 g / 6 oz / 1 ¾ cups rolled buckwheat flakes

100 g / 3 ½ oz / ¾ cup hazelnuts

75 g / 2 ½ oz / 2/3 cup almonds

100 g / 3 ½ oz / 1 cup sunflower seeds

150 g / 5 ½ oz / ¾ cup dried sour cherries

75 g / 2 ½ oz / 1/3 cup sultanas

soya yogurt to serve

METHOD

- Preheat the oven to 160°C (140°C fan) / 325F / gas 3.
- Stir the maple syrup, grape juice and oil together in a bowl with a pinch of salt then toss it with the buckwheat flakes, hazelnuts, almonds and sunflower seeds.
- Spread the mixture out on a large baking tray and bake for 1 hour, stirring every 10 minutes to ensure it all toasts evenly. Leave the granola to cool completely, then stir in the sour cherries and sultanas.
- Store in an airtight jar until needed, then serve with soya yogurt.

Mains

Eating clean, untreated produce can help you feel good. Following this regime does not limit the creativity or variety of meal choice. Whether you desire a lighter meal, such as the **Roasted Broccoli Salad**, or a full-blown dinnertime option along the lines of the **Spiced Grilled Salmon**, there are plenty of options in the following recipes. It is possibly easier than you anticipated to avoid processed and refined foods or those where preservatives or emulsifiers have been added, and still enjoy a wholesome, interesting meal experience. Choosing ingredients for soups, salads and stews packed with fresh, seasonal food has never been so satisfying!
Get creative with chosen produce – even buy local, where possible – and incorporate all kinds of ingredients you may not have considered in the past.
Prepare to eat your way to a healthy lifestyle!

Tomato Courgetti

SERVES: 4 - PREP. TIME: **10 MINS** / COOKING TIME: **0 MINS**

INGREDIENTS

4 small courgettes (zucchini)

2 avocados, peeled, stoned and sliced

225 g / 8 oz / 1 ½ cups cherry tomatoes, halved

½ red onion, sliced

2 tbsp flat-leaf parsley, chopped

FOR THE DRESSING:

3 tbsp extra virgin olive oil

1 tbsp cider vinegar

1 tsp runny honey

METHOD

- Use a spiraliser to turn the courgettes into spaghetti-like ribbons.

- Toss with the avocado, tomatoes, onion and parsley and divide between four bowls.

- Make a simple dressing by shaking the oil, vinegar and honey together in a small jar. Season with salt and pepper and serve with the salads.

Quinoa and Mackerel Salad

SERVES: **4** - PREP. TIME: **30 MINS** / COOKING TIME: **25 MINS**

INGREDIENTS

150 g / 5 ½ oz / ¾ cup black quinoa

3 tbsp extra virgin olive oil

1 lemon, juiced and zest finely grated

½ tsp chilli (chili) flakes

1 clove of garlic, crushed

2 tsp runny honey

2 tbsp baby capers

150 g / 5 ½ oz / 4 ½ cups baby chard leaves

2 smoked mackerel fillets, skinned, boned and flaked

METHOD

- Put the quinoa in a saucepan with 350 ml water. Cover and simmer gently for 10 minutes, then leave to stand off the heat for a further 15 minutes without lifting the lid.

- Whisk the olive oil, lemon juice and zest, chilli flakes, garlic, honey and capers in a bowl and season to taste with salt and pepper.

- Stir the quinoa into the dressing and leave to cool to room temperature.

- Toss the quinoa with the baby chard leaves and flaked smoked mackerel, then divide between four plates and serve immediately.

Lentil and Vegetable Soup

SERVES: **6** - PREP. TIME: **5 MINS** / COOKING TIME: **40 MINS**

INGREDIENTS

3 tbsp extra virgin olive oil

1 onion, quartered and sliced

2 cloves of garlic, crushed

1 tsp ground coriander

1 tsp ground cumin

½ tsp smoked paprika

1 carrot, peeled and diced

¼ white cabbage, chopped

200 g / 7 oz / 1 cup red lentils

200 g / 7 oz / 1 cup green lentils

1.2 litres / 2 pint / 5 cups fresh vegetable stock

1 small handful flat-leaf parsley, chopped

METHOD

- Heat the oil in a large saucepan and fry the onion for 5 minutes. Add the garlic and fry for 2 minutes. Stir in the spices, then add the vegetables and lentils and stir well to coat.

- Pour in the stock and cook over a high heat until it starts to boil.

- Reduce the heat and simmer for 30 minutes or until the lentils are tender. Season to taste with salt and pepper.

- Ladle the soup into warm bowls and sprinkle with parsley.

Tofu and Pak Choi Stir-fry

SERVES: 4 - PREP. TIME: 5 MINS / COOKING TIME: 8 MINS

INGREDIENTS

2 tbsp coconut oil

350 g / 12 oz / 1 ½ cups firm tofu, cubed

2 cloves of garlic, crushed

1 tsp fresh root ginger, finely grated

1 red chilli (chili), finely chopped

100 g / 3 ½ oz / 1 cup mangetout

3 pak choi, sliced

2 tbsp soy sauce

3 tbsp orange juice

50 g / 1 ¾ oz / ½ cup raw cashew nuts, roughly chopped

METHOD

- Heat the oil in a large wok and brown the tofu on all sides. Transfer to a warm plate and set aside.
- Add the garlic, ginger and chilli to the wok and stir-fry for 1 minute, then add the mangetout and pak choi and stir-fry for 2 minutes.
- Pour in the soy and orange juice, then return the tofu to the wok and stir fry for 1 minute.
- Sprinkle in the cashew nuts and serve immediately.

Salmon with Cucumber Salsa

SERVES: 4 - PREP. TIME: 5 MINS / COOKING TIME: 6 MINS

INGREDIENTS

4 portions salmon fillet

3 tbsp extra virgin olive oil

½ lemon, juiced

2 tsp runny honey

½ cucumber, seeds removed, flesh diced

8 radishes, diced

1 apple, cored and diced

1 celery stick, diced

1 small bunch flat leaf parsley, finely chopped

METHOD

- Heat the grill to its highest setting. Season the salmon with salt and pepper, then grill for 3 minutes on each side or until just cooked through.
- Whisk the oil, lemon and honey together with a pinch of salt and pepper, then toss with the cucumber, radish, apple, celery and parsley.
- Serve the salmon with the salsa spooned over the top.

Fresh Pea Soup

SERVES: 4 - PREP. TIME: **10 MINS** / COOKING TIME: **30 MINS**

INGREDIENTS

2 tbsp extra virgin olive oil

1 leek, chopped

2 cloves of garlic, crushed

1 large potato, peeled and diced

1 litre / 1 pint 14 fl. oz / 4 cups fresh vegetable stock

200 g / 7 oz / 1 1/3 cups fresh peas, podded weight

50 g / 1 ¾ oz / 1 ½ cups pea shoots

METHOD

- Heat the oil in a saucepan and fry the leeks for 8 minutes or until softened.
- Add the garlic and potato to the pan and cook for 2 more minutes, then pour in the stock.
- Simmer for 15 minutes, then stir in three quarters of the peas and cook for 3 minutes.
- Transfer the soup to a liquidiser with half of the pea shoots and blend until smooth. Season to taste with salt and black pepper.
- Pour the soup into four bowls and garnish with the rest of the peas and pea shoots.

Spicy Salad Wraps

SERVES: **4** - PREP. TIME: **10 MINS** / COOKING TIME: **20 MINS**

INGREDIENTS

150 g / 5 ½ oz / 1 cup ripe tomatoes,
chopped

1 tbsp coconut sugar

1 tbsp cider vinegar

1 tsp smoked paprika

100 ml / 3 ½ fl. oz / ½ cup soya yogurt

2 gherkins, finely chopped

1 spring onion (scallion), finely chopped

½ tbsp capers, finely chopped

4 wholegrain or gluten-free tortillas

75 g / 2 ½ oz / 2 ¼ cups rocket (arugula)

12 cherry tomatoes, halved

200 g / 7 oz / 1 cup canned sweetcorn,
drained

4 slices red pepper

4 green chillies (chilies), sliced

METHOD

- To make the ketchup, put the tomatoes in a saucepan with the sugar, vinegar and paprika. Cook, covered, until the mixture starts to boil, then reduce the heat and simmer uncovered for 15 minutes. Blend until smooth and leave to cool.

- To make the yogurt dressing, combine the yogurt with the gherkins, spring onion and capers and set aside.

- Lay out the tortillas and top with rocket, tomatoes, sweetcorn, pepper and chillies. Serve with the ketchup and yogurt dressing for drizzling over or dipping into.

Couscous Bean Salad

SERVES: **4** - PREP. TIME: **10 MINS** / COOKING TIME: **35 MINS**

INGREDIENTS

200 g / 7 oz extra-firm tofu, in 1 piece

1 tbsp sea salt

300 g / 10 ½ oz / 1 ¾ cups couscous

400 g / 14 oz / 2 cups canned mixed beans, rinsed and drained

200 g / 7 oz / 1 cup canned sweetcorn, rinsed and drained

¼ broccoli, grated

50 g / 1 ¾ oz / ¼ cup sultanas

4 tbsp extra virgin olive oil

2 limes, juiced

1 tsp runny honey

300 g / 10 ½ oz / 2 cups edamame (soya) beans, defrosted if frozen

1 handful micro herbs

METHOD

- Sprinkle the tofu all over with salt, then sandwich it between two double layers of kitchen paper and weigh it down with a heavy wooden chopping board. Leave for 2 hours or preferably overnight.
- Cook the couscous according to the packet instructions and leave to cool. Toss the couscous with the beans, sweetcorn, grated broccoli and sultanas.
- Whisk the oil with the lime juice and honey and season to taste with salt and pepper. Stir half of the dressing into the salad.
- Boil the edamame for 5 minutes or until tender, then plunge into iced water to cool. Drain well.
- Crumble the salted tofu and toss with the edamame, micro herbs and the rest of the dressing. Serve with the bean and couscous salad.

Spiced Grilled Salmon

SERVES: 4 - PREP. TIME: 30 MINS / COOKING TIME: 6 MINS

INGREDIENTS

4 salmon steaks, halved and boned

1 lime, sliced

2 tsp chilli (chili) flakes

FOR THE SPICE PASTE:

2 cloves of garlic, chopped

1 tbsp fresh root ginger, chopped

30 g / 1 oz / 1 cup Thai basil, leaves only, plus extra to garnish

30 g / 1 oz / 1 cup coriander (cilantro), leaves only

2 green chillies (chilies), chopped

2 tbsp cashew nuts

1 lime, zest finely grated

3 tbsp extra virgin olive oil

METHOD

- Soak eight wooden skewers in water for 20 minutes before using to stop them from burning.
- To make the spice paste, put all of the ingredients in a food processor and blend until smooth.
- Thread the salmon onto the skewers and brush them all over with the paste. Any unused paste can be served in a small bowl alongside for dipping.
- Arrange the salmon skewers and lime slices on a grill tray and cook under a very hot grill for 3 minutes on each side or until golden brown.
- Serve the salmon with a small bowl of chilli flakes for sprinkling over at the table.

MAINS

Roasted Broccoli Salad

SERVES: **4** - PREP. TIME: **10 MINS** / COOKING TIME: **25 MINS**

INGREDIENTS

1 head of broccoli, cut into florets

4 tbsp extra virgin olive oil

¼ tsp ground cumin

¼ tsp ground coriander

200 g / 7 oz / 1 cup canned chickpeas, rinsed and drained

100 g / 3 ½ oz / 3 cups baby leaf spinach

2 mild red chillies (chilies), sliced

FOR THE DRESSING:

1 tsp tahini paste

1 tsp runny honey

1 tbsp lemon juice

1 clove of garlic, crushed

50 ml / 1 ¾ fl. oz / ¼ cup soya yogurt

METHOD

- Preheat the oven to 200°C (180°C fan) / 400F / gas 6.

- Arrange the broccoli in a single layer in a large roasting tin. Drizzle it with half of the oil and sprinkle with salt, pepper and the ground spices. Roast the broccoli for 25 minutes, turning halfway through.

- Meanwhile, make the dressing. Dissolve the tahini and honey in the lemon juice, then incorporate the garlic and yogurt. Season to taste with salt.

- When the broccoli is ready, toss it with the chickpeas, spinach and chillies and divide between four bowls. Drizzle over the dressing and serve immediately.

Roasted Squash Salad

SERVES: 4 - PREP. TIME: **10 MINS** / COOKING TIME: **40 MINS**

INGREDIENTS

1 butternut squash, peeled, seeded and cut into fingers
3 tbsp extra virgin olive oil
1 tsp cumin seeds
4 plum tomatoes, quartered
100 g / 3 ½ oz / ¾ cup pecan nuts
½ lemon, zest finely grated
½ lime, zest finely grated
1 handful coriander (cilantro) leaves, chopped

FOR THE DRESSING:
1 tsp tahini paste
1 tsp runny honey
1 tbsp lemon juice
1 tbsp lime juice
1 clove of garlic, crushed
50 ml / 1 ¾ fl. oz / ¼ cup soya yogurt

METHOD

- Preheat the oven to 200°C (180°C fan) / 400F / gas 6.
- Arrange the squash in a single layer in a large roasting tin. Drizzle it with oil and sprinkle with salt, pepper and cumin seeds. Roast the squash for 40 minutes, turning it over and adding the tomatoes halfway through.
- Meanwhile, make the dressing. Dissolve the tahini and honey in the lemon and lime juice, then incorporate the garlic and yogurt. Season to taste with salt.
- When the squash is tender, divide it between four plates and scatter over the pecans, citrus zest and coriander. Drizzle with dressing and serve immediately.

Desserts

It is always enjoyable to finish off a meal with a delicious dessert and there's no exception to that once a Clean Eating style of diet has been adopted. The following recipes offer an assorted array of ways in which to enhance the sweeter flavours associated with desserts but using natural sweetness. Clean baking means being able to experience the joys of a baked dish without the use of dairy products and the inventive, creative ideas here will fill you with inspiration. Ditching dairy has never been more fun! Whether the refreshing **Strawberry Verrines** take your fancy, or you prefer to satisfy your sweet tooth with some **Black Bean Brownies**, there is something in here for every dessert-lover. If sweet foods aren't your thing but you still need that extra something after your main meal, the **Oat and Coconut Loaf Cake** is a treat that will definitely hit the spot! The flourish of a yummy dessert to end a meal is a satisfying and enjoyable one, and often the most anticipated course. Savour every bite and appreciate the fresh ingredients even more.

Matcha Brownies

MAKES: **9** - PREP. TIME: **20 MINS** / COOKING TIME: **35 MINS**

INGREDIENTS

225 g / 8 oz / 1 ½ cups gluten-free plain (all-purpose) flour

½ tsp baking powder

1 ½ tbsp matcha green tea powder

1 tbsp pure cacao powder

185 g / 6 ½ oz / ¾ cup unsweetened apple puree

150 g / 5 ½ oz / ¾ cup coconut sugar

100 ml / 3 ½ fl. oz / ½ cup coconut oil, melted

75 ml / 2 ½ oz / 1/3 cup coconut milk

1 tsp vanilla extract

FOR THE ICING:

100 g / 3 ½ oz / 1 cup coconut flour

1 tbsp runny honey

METHOD

- Preheat the oven to 180°C (160°C fan) / 350F / gas 4 and oil and line a 20 cm (8 in) square cake tin with greaseproof paper.
- Mix together the flour, baking powder, matcha and cacao in a large mixing bowl and set aside.
- Beat the rest of the ingredients together in a separate bowl, then fold the wet mixture into the dry ingredients until just combined.
- Scrape the mixture into the prepared tin and level the surface. Bake for 35 minutes or until just set in the centre. Leave to cool completely in the tin before cutting into squares.
- Mix the coconut flour with the honey to make a thick pipeable icing, adding a few drops of water if necessary. Spoon it into a piping bag and pipe a few lines across each brownie.

Balsamic Baked Figs

SERVES: 4 - PREP. TIME: **5 MINS** / COOKING TIME: **15 MINS**

INGREDIENTS

4 fresh figs, halved
1 tbsp balsamic vinegar

METHOD

- Preheat the oven to 200°C (180°C fan) / 400F / gas 6 and line a baking tray with greaseproof paper.
- Arrange the figs cut side up on the baking tray and drizzle with balsamic vinegar.
- Bake the figs for 15 minutes and serve warm.

Raw Berry Cheesecake

SERVES: 6 - PREP. TIME: **45 MINS** / FREEZING TIME: **4 HOURS**

INGREDIENTS

150 g / 5 oz / 1 cup mixed frozen berries, defrosted

2 tbsp coconut sugar

250 g / 9 oz / 1 ½ cups medjool dates, stoned

225 g / 8 oz / 2 ¼ cups ground almonds

250 g / 9 oz / 1 2/3 cups raw cashew nuts, soaked overnight

400 ml / 14 fl. oz / 2 cup canned coconut milk, chilled unopened

1 ½ lemons, juiced and zest finely grated

75 ml / 2 ½ fl. oz / 1/3 cup maple syrup

50 ml 1 ¾ oz / ¼ cup runny honey

¼ tsp nutmeg, freshly grated

METHOD

- Mix the berries with the coconut sugar and leave to macerate for 20 minutes.
- Soak the dates in warm water for 10 minutes, then drain and blend to a smooth paste in a food processor. Add the ground almonds and pulse until it forms a dough. Line a 20 cm (8 in) round spring-form cake tin with clingfilm, then press the mixture into the base.
- Drain the cashews and put them in the food processor. Open the can of coconut milk upside down and discard the thin watery layer. Scoop the thick creamy layer into the food processor and add the lemon juice, zest and maple syrup.
- Blend until very smooth, pausing to scrape down the sides occasionally.
- Spoon half of the macerated berries over the cheesecake base and top with the cashew mixture. Cover with clingfilm and freeze for at least 4 hours.
- Remove from the freezer 20 minutes before serving. Unmould the cheesecake and cut into wedges. Mix the honey with the nutmeg and drizzle over the top, then serve with the rest of the berries on the side.

Chocolate Raspberry Tarts

MAKES: 8 - PREP. TIME: 35 MINS / COOKING TIME: 3 HOURS

INGREDIENTS

FOR THE CRUST:

250 g / 9 oz / 1 2/3 cups blanched almonds

25 g / 1 oz / ¼ cup pure cacao powder

2 tbsp coconut flour

50 ml / 1 ¾ fl. oz / ¼ cup maple syrup

3 tbsp coconut oil, melted

FOR THE FILLING:

150 g / 5 oz / 1 cup raspberries

225 ml / 8 fl. oz / ¾ cup canned coconut milk

300 g / 10 ½ oz / 2 cups dark chocolate (min 85% cocoa solids), finely chopped

2 tbsp coconut oil

coconut flour for sprinkling

METHOD

- Put the almonds, cacao and coconut flour in a food processor and process until finely ground. Add the maple syrup and coconut oil and pulse until it forms a dough. Press the dough into the base and sides of eight small tart moulds.

- Reserve eight raspberries and mash the rest with a fork. Spoon a little into each mould.

- Put the coconut milk in a small saucepan with a pinch of salt and heat it gently. Meanwhile, put the chocolate and coconut oil in a mixing bowl.

- When the coconut milk starts to simmer, pour it over the chocolate in the bowl. Leave it to stand for 30 seconds, then stir gently until it forms a homogenous smooth ganache.

- Divide the ganache between the moulds then chill for 3 hours or until set.

- Garnish each tart with a raspberry and a sprinkle of coconut flour.

Coconut and Raspberry Fool

SERVES: **4** - PREP. TIME: **10 MINS** / COOKING TIME: **0 MINS**

INGREDIENTS

400 ml / 14 fl. oz / 2 cup canned coconut milk, chilled unopened

2 tbsp coconut sugar

150 g / 5 oz / 1 cup raspberries

1 tbsp runny honey

mint leaves to garnish

METHOD

- Open the can of coconut milk upside down and discard the thin watery layer. Scoop the thick creamy layer into a bowl and add the coconut sugar.
- Whip with an electric whisk until it reaches the consistency of whipped cream.
- Mash the raspberries with the honey and divide between four small glasses.
- Top with the coconut cream and ripple together lightly with a spoon. Serve immediately, garnished with mint.

Blueberry Crumbles

MAKES: 6 - PREP. TIME: 15 MINS / COOKING TIME: 25 MINS

INGREDIENTS

350 g / 12 ½ oz / 2 1/3 cups blueberries

2 tbsp maple syrup

75 g / 2 ½ oz / 1/3 cup coconut oil

75 g / 2 ½ oz / ½ cup buckwheat flour

25 g / 1 oz / ¼ cup rolled buckwheat flakes

25 g / 1 oz / ¼ cup ground almonds

40 g / 1 ½ oz / ¼ cup coconut sugar

lemon balm to garnish

METHOD

- Preheat the oven to 180°C (160°C fan) / 350F / gas 4.
- Reserve a few of the berries for decoration, then mix the rest with the maple syrup and divide them between six ramekin dishes.
- Rub the coconut oil into the buckwheat flour then stir in the buckwheat flakes, ground almonds and coconut sugar.
- Crumble the mixture over the blueberries then bake for 25 minutes or until the topping is brown and crisp.
- Garnish with the reserved berries and lemon balm just before serving.

Tropical Fruit Sorbet

SERVES: **6** - PREP. TIME: **10 MINS** / FREEZING TIME: **3-4 HOURS**

INGREDIENTS

2 ripe mangoes, peeled, stoned and chopped

2 ripe papaya, peeled, seeded and chopped

2 passion fruit, pulp sieved and seeds discarded

1 banana, peeled and chopped

100 ml / 3 ½ fl. oz / ½ cup pure pineapple juice

50 g / 1 ¾ oz / ¼ cup coconut sugar

mint sprigs or lemon balm to garnish

METHOD

• Put all of the ingredients, except the herbs, in a liquidiser and blend until very smooth.

• Churn in an ice cream maker, according to the manufacturer's instructions, then freeze for 2 hours.

• Alternatively, scrape the mixture into a plastic box with a lid and freeze for 2 hours. Scrape the semi-frozen mixture into a food processor and blend until smooth, then return it to the box and freeze for 1 hour. Whiz the mixture in the food processor again, then freeze until firm.

• Scoop the sorbet into glasses and garnish with mint or lemon balm.

Black Bean Brownies

MAKES: **9** - PREP. TIME: **10 MINS** / COOKING TIME: **20 MINS**

INGREDIENTS

50 g / 1 ¾ oz / ½ cup rolled porridge oats

2 tbsp pure cacao powder

1 tsp baking powder

400 g / 14 oz / 2 cups canned black beans, drained and rinsed

100 ml / 3 ½ fl. oz / ½ cup maple syrup

50 ml / 1 ¾ oz / ¼ cup coconut oil, melted

1 vanilla pod, seeds only

100 g / 3 ½ oz / 2/3 cup dark chocolate (minimum 85 % cocoa solids), finely chopped

METHOD

- Preheat the oven to 180°C (160°C fan) / 350F / gas 4 and oil and line a 20 cm (8 in) square cake tin with greaseproof paper.
- Put the oats, cacao and baking powder in a food processor and blitz to a powder. Add the black beans, maple syrup, coconut oil and vanilla and blend again until very smooth.
- Fold in the chopped chocolate, then scrape the mixture into the tin and level the top.
- Bake for 20 minutes or until the outside is set, but the centre is still quite soft. Leave the brownie to cool completely before cutting and serving.

Strawberry Verrines

SERVES: **4** - PREP. TIME: **15 MINS** / COOKING TIME: **0 MINS**

INGREDIENTS

400 ml / 14 fl. oz / 2 cup canned coconut milk, chilled unopened

2 tbsp runny honey

1 tsp vanilla extract

250 ml / 9 fl. oz / 1 cup soya yogurt

100 g / 3 ½ oz / ¾ cup healthy granola

30 g / 1 oz / ¼ cup raw cocoa nibs

150 g / 5 oz / 1 cup strawberries, half sliced, half quartered

4 sprigs mint

METHOD

- Open the can of coconut milk upside down and discard the thin watery layer. Scoop the thick creamy layer into a bowl and add the honey and vanilla extract.
- Whip with an electric whisk until it reaches the consistency of whipped cream, then fold in the yogurt.
- Divide a third of the mixture between four glasses. Mix the granola and cocoa nibs together and scatter half over the top, then arrange the sliced strawberries around the inside of the glasses.
- Top with the rest of the coconut mixture then garnish with the rest of the granola, the quartered strawberries and mint sprigs.

Hazelnut Cookies

MAKES: 12 - PREP. TIME: 20 MINS / COOKING TIME: 20 MINS

INGREDIENTS

100 g / 3 ½ oz / 1 cup rolled buckwheat flakes

150 g / 5 ½ oz / 1 cup buckwheat flour

75 g / 2 ½ oz / 2/3 cup hazelnuts, chopped

50 g / 1 ¾ oz / ½ cup desiccated coconut

100 g / 3 ½ oz / ½ cup coconut sugar

½ tsp bicarbonate of (baking) soda

125 ml / 4 ½ fl. oz / ½ cup coconut oil, melted

METHOD

- Preheat the oven to 180°C (160° fan) / 350F / gas 4 and line a large baking tray with greaseproof paper.
- Put all of the ingredients in a food processor and pulse until it forms a dough, adding a few tbsp of water if necessary.
- Roll the mixture into walnut-sized balls, then flatten them onto the baking tray.
- Transfer the tray to the oven and bake for 20 minutes, turning round halfway though. Leave to cool completely on the tray before serving.

Oat and Coconut Loaf Cake

SERVES: **8** - PREP. TIME: **15 MINS** / COOKING TIME: **50 MINS**

INGREDIENTS

150 g / 5 ½ oz / 1 cup gluten-free plain (all-purpose) flour

125 g / 4 ½ oz / 1 ¼ cups rolled porridge oats

50 g / 1 ¾ oz / ½ cup desiccated or flaked coconut

1 tsp bicarbonate of (baking) soda

3 very ripe bananas

50 ml / 1 ¾ fl. oz / ¼ cup coconut milk

50 ml / 1 ¾ fl. oz / ¼ cup coconut oil, melted

75 ml / 2 ½ fl. oz / 1/3 cup runny honey

250 g / 9 oz / 1 ½ cup cooked quinoa

coconut butter to serve

METHOD

- Preheat the oven to 180°C (160°C fan) / 350F / gas 4 and oil and line a large loaf tin with greaseproof paper.
- Mix together the flour, oats, coconut and baking soda in a large mixing bowl and set aside.
- Mash the bananas in a separate bowl, then beat in the coconut milk, oil, honey and quinoa.
- Fold the wet ingredients into the dry ingredients until just combined, then scrape into the tin.
- Bake for 50 minutes or until a skewer inserted in the centre comes out clean. Leave to cool on a wire rack, then slice and serve with coconut butter for spreading.

Sides & Snacks

Food that is free from all additives does not mean skimping on flavour and fulfilment but it still may not stop the longing for a snack now and again. There are plenty of options for deliciously clean snacks with this diet regime, and the range of enticing side dishes is inspirational – some of which are shown in this chapter. Whether you want a hot choice for a side or a simple cold option to take on a day out, the ways in which your natural produce can work are endless. The nutritious, protein-packed **Date and Almond Cacao Balls** are fantastic for eating on the go, or the **Banana Bread** is great as an afternoon snack or a treat to share with friends. Clean, yet creative side dishes and satisfying snacks can easily be achieved because the food you are using is natural, unrefined and pure; the perfect dietary health-giving combination.

Avocado Hummus

SERVES: 4 - PREP. TIME: **10 MINS** / COOKING TIME: **0 MINS**

INGREDIENTS

1 small bunch flat-leaf parsley, leaves only

200 g / 7 oz / 1 cup canned chickpeas (garbanzo beans), drained

2 ripe avocados, peeled and stoned

4 tbsp extra virgin olive oil

1 tbsp tahini paste

1 lemon, juiced

1 clove of garlic, crushed

¼ tsp ground coriander

METHOD

- Reserve one parsley leaf for the garnish and put the rest in a food processor with the rest of the ingredients.
- Blend to a smooth puree, then season to taste with salt and pepper.
- Spoon into a bowl and garnish with the reserved parsley leaf.

Spinach and Strawberry Salad

SERVES: **4** - PREP. TIME: **2 HOURS 15 MINS** / COOKING TIME: **0 MINS**

INGREDIENTS

200 g / 7 oz extra-firm tofu, in 1 piece

1 tbsp sea salt

150 g / 5 ½ oz / 4 ½ cups baby leaf spinach

150 g / 5 ½ oz / 1 cup strawberries, sliced

30 g / 1 oz / ½ cup almonds, roughly chopped

3 tbsp extra virgin olive oil

2 tbsp balsamic vinegar

1 tsp runny honey

1 clove of garlic, crushed

METHOD

- Sprinkle the tofu all over with the salt, then sandwich it between two double layers of kitchen paper and weigh it down with a heavy wooden chopping board. Leave for 2 hours or preferably overnight.
- Divide the spinach between four bowls and scatter over the strawberries and almonds.
- Whisk the oil, vinegar, honey and garlic together with a pinch of salt and drizzle over the salad.
- Crumble the salted tofu over the salad and add plenty of freshly ground black pepper.

Beetroot Hummus Toasts

SERVES: 4 - PREP. TIME: 2 HOURS 15 MINS / COOKING TIME: 0 MINS

INGREDIENTS

200 g / 7 oz extra-firm tofu, in 1 piece

1 tbsp sea salt

4 tbsp extra virgin olive oil

200 g / 7 oz / 1 cup canned chickpeas (garbanzo beans), drained

2 cooked beetroot

1 tbsp tahini paste

1 lemon, juiced

1 clove of garlic, crushed

¼ tsp ground cumin

4 slices gluten-free bread, cut into triangles

2 courgettes (zucchini), sliced into ribbons with a vegetable peeler

1 small bunch flat-leaf parsley

METHOD

- Sprinkle the tofu all over with the salt, then sandwich it between two double layers of kitchen paper and weigh it down with a heavy wooden chopping board. Leave for 2 hours or preferably overnight.
- Put half the oil in a food processor with the chickpeas, beetroot, tahini, lemon juice, garlic and cumin.
- Blend to a smooth puree, then season to taste with salt and pepper.
- Toast the bread and drizzle it with the rest of the oil, then top with the beetroot hummus. Arrange the courgette ribbons on top, then crumble over the tofu and garnish with plenty of parsley.

Kale Chips

SERVES: 4 - PREP. TIME: **5 MINS** / COOKING TIME: **30 MINS**

INGREDIENTS

2 tbsp extra virgin olive oil

100 g / 3 ½ oz / 3 cups kale, washed and dried

25 g / 1 oz / 1/4 cup linseeds

METHOD

- Preheat the oven to 150°C (130°C fan) / 300F / gas 2.
- Massage the oil into the kale and spread it out in a roasting tin.
- Sprinkle with linseeds and season lightly with salt, then roast for 30 minutes, stirring every 10 minutes.

Date and Almond Cacao Balls

MAKES: **12** - PREP. TIME: **15 MINS** / CHILLING TIME: **1 HOUR**

INGREDIENTS

125 g / 4 ½ oz / 1 cup blanched almonds

100 g / 3 ½ oz / 1 cup desiccated coconut

2 tbsp runny honey

75 g / 2 ½ oz / 1/3 cup almond butter

30 g / 1 oz / ¼ cup pure cacao powder

8 medjool dates, stoned and chopped

METHOD

• Put the almonds and coconut in a food processor and blitz until finely ground. Add the rest of the ingredients and pulse to form a dough.

• Divide the dough into 12 equal pieces and roll each one into a ball.

• Chill in the fridge for 1 hour before serving.

Mixed-seed Scones

MAKES: **12** - PREP. TIME: **25 MINS** / COOKING TIME: **12 MINS**

INGREDIENTS

150 g / 5 ½ oz / 1 cup gluten-free
self-raising flour

75 g / 2 ½ oz / ½ cup buckwheat flour

1 tsp baking powder

55 g / 2 oz / ¼ cup coconut oil

75 g / 2 ½ oz / 1/3 cup mixed seeds

50 g / 1 ¾ oz / ¼ cup goji berries

2 tbsp currants

150 ml / 5 fl. oz / 2/3 cup almond milk, plus
a little extra for brushing

METHOD

- Preheat the oven to 220°C (200°C fan) / 425F / gas 7 and oil a large baking sheet.
- Sieve the flours and baking powder into a bowl and rub in the coconut oil until the mixture resembles fine breadcrumbs.
- Mix the seeds with the goji berries and currants. Set half aside for the topping and stir the rest into the flour.
- Stir in enough milk to bring the mixture together into a soft dough. Flatten the dough with your hands on a floured work surface until 2.5 cm (1 in) thick.
- Use a pastry cutter to cut out 12 circles and transfer them to the prepared baking sheet, then brush with almond milk and top with the rest of the seed mix.
- Bake in the oven for 12 minutes or until golden brown and cooked through. Transfer the scones to a wire rack to cool completely.

Beetroot and Walnut Dip

SERVES: **2** - PREP. TIME: **20 MINS** / COOKING TIME: **0 MINS**

INGREDIENTS

75 g / 2 ½ oz / ½ cup walnuts, chopped

2 cooked beetroot

100 g / 3 ½ oz / ½ cup silken tofu

2 tbsp walnut oil

2 tbsp lemon juice

2 tbsp fresh dill, chopped

METHOD

- Reserve 1 tbsp of walnuts for the garnish and soak the rest in warm water for 15 minutes.
- Drain well, then transfer to a food processor with the beetroot, tofu, walnut oil, lemon juice and half of the dill. Blitz until very smooth, pausing to scrape down the sides occasionally.
- Season to taste with salt and black pepper, then spoon into a serving bowl and garnish with the reserved walnuts and dill.

Banana Bread

SERVES: 8 - PREP. TIME: 15 MINS / COOKING TIME: 50 MINS

INGREDIENTS

125 g / 4 ½ oz / 1 ¼ cups rolled porridge oats

125 g / 4 ½ oz / 1 ¼ cups ground almonds

100 g / 3 ½ oz / ½ cup coconut sugar

200 g / 7 oz / 1 1/3 cups gluten-free plain (all-purpose) flour

3 tsp baking powder

3 very ripe bananas, mashed

1 egg, beaten

175 ml / 6 fl. oz / 2/3 cup soya milk

50 ml / 1 ¾ fl. oz / ¼ cup coconut oil, melted

sliced bananas to serve

METHOD

- Preheat the oven to 180°C (160°C fan) / 350F / gas 4 and oil and line a large loaf tin with greaseproof paper.

- Put the oats in a food processor and blitz to a powder. Add the ground almonds, coconut sugar, flour and baking powder and blend again briefly to mix.

- Add the bananas, egg, soya milk and coconut oil and pulse until smoothly combined, then scrape into the tin.

- Bake for 50 minutes or until a skewer inserted in the centre comes out clean. Leave to cool completely on a wire rack before slicing and serving with sliced banana.

Chilled Borscht

SERVES: 4 - PREP. TIME: **5 MINS** / COOKING TIME: **0 MINS**

INGREDIENTS

4 cooked beetroot, cubed

½ cucumber, peeled, seeded and cubed

600 ml / 1 pint / 2 ½ cups fresh vegetable stock

250 ml / 9 fl. oz / 1 cup apple juice

1 tbsp cider vinegar

3 tbsp extra virgin olive oil

TO GARNISH:

¼ cucumber, diced

4 radishes, diced

4 beetroot or baby chard leaves

METHOD

- Put all of the soup ingredients in a liquidiser and blend until smooth.
- Season to taste with salt and pepper, then blend again.
- Chill in the fridge until ready to serve, then pour into glasses and garnish with cucumber, radish and beetroot leaves.

Spiced Chickpeas

SERVES: **4** - PREP. TIME: **5 MINS** / COOKING TIME: **30 MINS**

INGREDIENTS

400 g / 14 oz / 2 cups canned chickpeas

1 tbsp extra virgin olive oil

½ tsp ground cumin

½ tsp ground coriander

½ tsp ground dried garlic

METHOD

- Preheat the oven to 200°C (180°C fan) / 400F / gas 6 and line a baking tray with greaseproof paper.

- Rinse the chickpeas then drain them and dry thoroughly with kitchen paper. Toss the chickpeas with the oil, spices and a pinch of salt, then spread them out on the baking tray.

- Roast in the oven for 35 minutes or until crisp, stirring occasionally.

Chia Crispbread Sandwiches

SERVES: 4 - PREP. TIME: 20 MINS / COOKING TIME: 55 MINS

INGREDIENTS

FOR THE CRISPBREADS:

75 g / 2 ½ oz / 1/3 cup chia seeds

75 g / 2 ½ oz / 1/3 cup golden linseeds seeds

75 g / 2 ½ oz / 1/3 cup sesame seeds

50 g / 1 ¾ oz / ½ cup ground almonds

1 tsp herbes de Provence

FOR THE FILLING:

100 g / 3 ½ oz / ½ cup hummus

100 g / 3 ½ oz / ½ cup vegan pesto

1 large handful rocket (arugula)

1 red pepper, sliced

35 g / 1 ¼ oz / 1 cup alfalfa sprouts

2 tbsp pine nuts, toasted

3 spring onions (scallions), chopped

METHOD

- Preheat the oven to 160°C (140°C fan) / 325F / gas 3 and line a large baking tray with greaseproof paper.
- Mix all of the crispbread ingredients in a bowl with ¼ tsp salt, then stir in 250 ml of cold water. When all of the water has been absorbed, spread it onto the baking tray in an even 5 mm thick layer.
- Bake the crispbread sheet for 30 minutes. Cut it into eight even rectangles, turn them over with a spatula, then return the tray to the oven and bake for 25 minutes or until dry and crisp. Leave to cool on the tray.
- Spread half of the crispbreads with hummus and the other half with pesto. Top the hummus breads with rocket, pepper, alfalfa sprouts, pine nuts and spring onions, then invert the pesto crispbreads on top.

Index